Zen Sto

Mulla Nasrudine

The Laughter Masters

by Connie Zareen Delaney

Copyright

Table of Contents

Contents

Just a bunch of stories.

Let's Get Started

Welcome to the Laughter Masters. My goal with this book is to save you from the spiritual search. Crazy idea, huh?

The reason is because life needs you. As long as you are *searching* for life, we don't have the full *you* participating here with the rest of us. We need you now.

You're Better Than You "Think"

My experience is that people on the spiritual search are some of the best people but too much is being wasted by long, lengthy, forever spiritual searches.

So, let's just go ahead and get it done.

How do you do that? The best way is with stories, because the human mind operates on stories. We are all crazy because we have been given ridiculous stories since birth. So, one of the best ways to wake up is to rewrite the story. We want to rewrite the story that tells you that you don't know who you are. We have deep societal stories that are telling us we are separate from the world. We have

7

religions that tell us that you must die in order to get to heaven.

We have other religions that tell us you can reach a thing called enlightenment, but it's going to take lifetimes and lifetimes and lifetimes to do it.

Undo It All

So. Let's dive through the stories, but let's not do it in a forever search. Because this is a doable thing.

I wouldn't have the goal of saving you from your spiritual search if I didn't know that the solution is right here. That we can find it. That you are capable of finding this.

And we need you. We need the full 100% you to be a full human being here on the planet with us right now.

We Got Some Cleanup to Do.

Humanity has this huge job to do, to clean up the mess that we've created. This mess has only been created in a handful of generations. It has been created so quickly that it's not really as deep a mess as you may think. Cleanup is doable.

Same thing with all the stories you've been told. The stories that make a mess in your brain. The stories that are keeping you from knowing who you are.

These stories can be undone, and you can find who you are.

Ordinariness

Our beginning Zen stories are about ordinariness. And just think… You don't have to strive for ordinariness. You don't have to look for that. All you have to do is relax because you are already it.

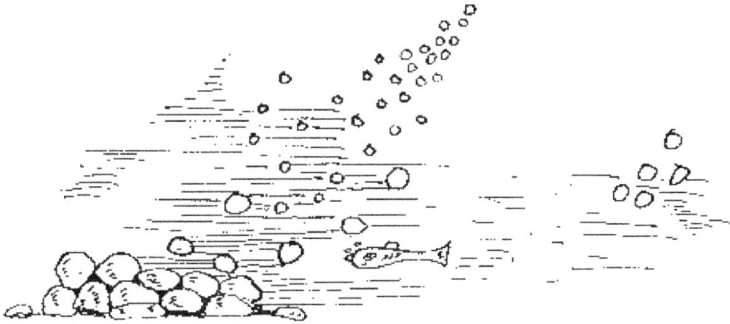

Bankai the Gardener

A long time ago in the land of Zen, there was a great master whose name was Bankai. He had a small ashram up in the mountains, and disciples would come traveling up to find him.

One day he was out working in the garden and such a fellow came along. This seeker walked up to Bankai and said, "Gardener. Where is the master? I have come to lay myself down at his feet."

Bankai looked up and said, "The Master, of course, is inside, sitting on the master's chair. Just go around the back of the hut. In through the back door and you will find him there."

So, the man strode away, walked around the hut and went in through the back door. There he saw Bankai, the gardener, sitting in the master's chair.

He was incensed, and he yelled, "Gardner, where's the master? What are you doing in his chair? This is sacrilegious."

Bankai looked at him and smiled, got down out of the chair and sat on the floor. But he said, "Now you will not find the master in the chair because the master is sitting on the floor."

The seeker was still mad; he couldn't admit his error. He stomped away and missed his opportunity.

> *This seeker didn't get it. He couldn't believe that a Master could be so ordinary – just a simple man in a garden.*

Mulla's Clothes

One day, Mulla Nasrudin showed up in a nearby town for an appointment, stark naked. Everyone was shocked.

They're like, "Mulla! What's the deal? What's going on?"

Mulla shrugged and said, "I was in such a hurry to get dressed, I forgot my clothes."

The ordinary spiritual teacher can be spacey too.

Everyone You Meet

This week's Zen stories are telling us that the enlightened master, the enlightened person, is a very simple ordinary person… in fact the enlightened person might be the only ordinary person.

This is the only person who is not hankering to become something else or pretending to be something else.

This is important to understand because we tend to get sucked in by beautiful charismatic religious teachers. This Zen story is the anecdote. The path is very different if we are looking for a totally ordinary person to guide us to enlightenment. Oure important than that... Our approach to life changes when we are looking to become ordinary, instead of some mystical magical person.

It's relaxing and easy to look for the most ordinary aspect of ourselves. That is who we are, who we always have been.

The Zen of it All

This is one of the reasons Zen stories are so important. They always seem to have a little funny twist to them, but they are telling important truths.

Like Mulla Nasruddin. He's basically a made-up guy. But he's useful for mystical stories. He forgot to wear his clothes. That's not how an enlightened teacher would behave. Right? That's pretty forgetful!

And we have Bankai, who was a very famous Zen master, and he is just so normal that he's out working in the garden. A new seeker comes along and doesn't recognize him. The gardener looks so normal and plain that he doesn't recognize him at all.

This and That

On one side this is important because it stops us from hankering after this magical mystical thing that is so glittery.

On the other hand, this makes everything pretty dang tricky. How the heck to you find a teacher? How you tell who is the most ordinary person around… because they are ordinary. They laugh when they laugh, they make mistakes when they make mistakes. Hopefully they pretty much wear clothes most the time.

Everyone I Meet

I have a little trick I would like to offer you. I made a decision a long time ago, after listening to Zen stories, to help me find the ordinary masters of the world. My rule is that everyone I meet, every time I meet someone, I decide they are enlightened already.

It saves me from having to decide, right? And who the heck am I to decide if someone is enlightened or not anyway?

Second of all, this is a good way to change my perspective about everyone. It makes life very, very simple, particularly in spiritual circles.

So, I decide that everyone that I meet is enlightened… until they convince me otherwise. Try that for a while and see how it makes your life different.

Bankai's Miracle

Here's another story about Bankai. One day he's sitting with his disciples quietly teaching. Having a moment, maybe a cup of tea. When a disciple of another sect comes walking up and he says, "Bankai. My master can stand on one side of the river with a brush in his hand and write a holy name on a piece of paper being held by another disciple on the far side of the river. Can you do that?"

Bankai looks at him and says, "I can only do one miracle. I can eat when I'm hungry, and sleep when I'm tired."

Ordinariness

What would it be like if we stopped looking for miracles? We might find reality! Reality is that place where perception is not broken.

This Zen story is another one about ordinariness. It's a story about Bankai from a long time ago, but we still do the same nonsense today. It's about how we are always hankering for miracles and magic.

Islam Includes This

An interesting tidbit about Mohammed, and tribal society at the time of Mohammed: They didn't like miracles either. The reason was that there were so many tricksters around who would pretend that they were making miracles and fool people.

As any good magician will tell you, it's easy to fake magic. It's easy to fake a miracle. There were so many fakers then, and there still are today. So, they didn't trust miracle making in a spiritual teacher. What they valued instead was poetry… because you can't fake good poetry.

Do we want magic?

So, this is something to think about. How much are we hankering after magic? Are we looking for something to come save us? We want prosperity, and healing or health. If we are looking for that it's easy to find fakers.

You find what you look for.

On the other hand, if we strive to discover the value of ordinariness – that totally changes our day-to-day life. All day long we are ordinary anyway! We're not that fabulous. It brings us close each time we remember.

Everyday Miracles

There is a lot of wisdom in finding miracles in everyday life. There's a point where we can see that all life is a miracle. But that is a totally different thing. I'm talking about hankering after a miracle. Believing that the spiritual master is going to be this magical being who swoops in and fills you with… whatever you are looking for: prosperity, or love or whatever.

Ordinariness is way easier. This is who we are. This is what makes us part of everything, not separate. A simple, ordinary part of everything.

It's one of the most valuable teachings of Zen.

The Three Sons

Once there was a king who had three sons. They were all really great. They had been trained by the finest teachers, and they had all grown into magnificent young men.

The oldest was the bravest. He hunted for bears in the high mountains. He brought back hides for rugs. He could challenge any man in the King's army and win.

The middle son was the tallest and the strongest. He stood a head above the king and could wrestle any challenger to the ground.

The youngest son was great all around. He was a good marksman. He was strong. He tended to be just a little bit of a dreamer. He was actually, very ordinary and didn't stand out in any way.

The king loved them all and appreciated their talents. But he needed to choose one to rule the Kingdom. So, he came upon an idea.

He ordered his sons to get their bows and accompany him down by the road. He walked out through an open field until he spied a vulture sitting up in a tree.

The King looks up at the vulture and then towards his three sons and says, "I want you to shoot that vulture."

He started with the eldest son. The eldest son was so strong and fierce. He grabbed his bow. He pulled it. Gets ready to shoot.

But the King shouts, "Stop. What do you see?"

The oldest son stops and says, "Well, I see grass, I see clouds, the sky, the river."

King says, "Stop, stop, stop. Never mind, never mind."

He then brings the second son up. He says, "I want you to shoot the vulture in the tree."

The second son jumps up enthusiastically, grabs his bow. He gets ready to shoot when the king stops him and says, "Wait. What do you see?"

"Ah," said the second son. "I see horses on the ground, a field of wheat and a dead tree with a vulture in it."

"Never mind," said the King. "Don't shoot it."

He looks at the third son and says, "I want you to shoot the vulture in the tree."

 The third son calmly gets his bow, pulls the string back and gets ready to shoot when the king stops him. He says, "Wait, stop. What do you see?"

The young man remained pointing at the tree and said, "I see the point where the wings join the body." and let the arrow fly. It hit square on and felled the vulture from the tree.

The third son became king.

* Don't worry about the Vulture. It's just a story.

The Straight Arrow Focus

Today's Zen story is on focus. What is that single point of reality that we come from? You find it when you are completely focused. Pro tip: Artists and musicians have that kind of focus!

The human mind is so amazing because it can wander to so many things. Imagination can be vivid and real. It's easy for our attention to be drawn from one thing to another. In fact, that's one of the things that distinguishes a child: the mind and imagination floats freely.

But when we are adults we are often divided. The capacity for imagination becomes like a split identity, floating from one shiny thing to another.

Lack of Focus

When you don't know who you are your attention is easily sucked off and you *become* the thing your attention is focused on. This can happen for outside or inside things.

You have an emotion, and it feels so compelling. It's like "I am this emotion." Particularly if it's a negative emotion, right? We get sucked into it and lose focus.

Awakening is like a focus point. Knowing who you are is finding this point of awareness inside ourselves. It is such a single point that it is dissolved into nothing. That's you seeing the world.

The King

This story is about a King. He has a couple of sons, and he brings the sons out to go hunting. Only one of his sons is able to focus so sharply on what he is shooting that he sees nothing else.

One cool point in this story is that this one son, the youngest son, was a dreamer. He was an artist, full of imagination. But he had learned how to focus his imagination.

The king knew the value of focus in a leader and made this son king.

Focus on Focus

Work on increasing focus. This is one of the reasons why learning how to play music is so valuable, because learning music requires lots of focus. It's a Zen practice.

The Crux of the Matter

In these beginning stories we are getting to the crux of why I am writing this book. It's about focus. But why would we need to focus?

So many spiritual teachings these days are like, "Everything's OK, everything's fine. Don't worry about anything."

I disagree. We should be worried. We should be very worried.

There are a lot of problems going on and we need to be the best and the brightest and the clearest and the most focused people possible to be working on these problems.

My teacher Osho always taught that if we want to change the world, we need a new human. We need a new humanity. The earth itself doesn't need changing. It's fine. It's people having a problem. And you and me? We are people.

Osho said the only way this can be done is if there are enough people with completely clear perception working together. He said there needs to be Ten Thousand Buddhas working together.

Imagine this kind of focus. Just like the focus we had in our Zen story on the three sons. The youngest son was so focused on the goal. Shooting the arrow. All you see is the point where the wing meets the chest.

That kind of focus. Yes.

Imagine ten thousand completely awake, focused people working on changing the world?

This is what I'm talking about. We have some real work to do and the thrill of doing it together is going to be amazing. We have so many children, so many people coming up behind us in the world. We need to create this for them.

Rinjai's Cat

A long time ago, back in the land of Zen, there was a monastery.

This monastery had two wings. There were 1000 monks in the monastery. Half of them, 500, were on one wing and half of them, 500, were on the other wing.

The master had this beautiful cat. The cat was so friendly. He would sometimes go to the east wing, and sometimes come back and go to the west wing.

All the monks loved to pet the cat. He was so soft and so beautiful. Each one of them wanted to keep it for themselves. They were constantly bickering over who got to have the cat.

Finally, the master had enough of this. He called everybody together into the big room. He said, "Listen. This cat has become a huge disturbance here in the monastery. So, here's what we're going to do. If anyone here can prove that he is a meditator, can prove that he has encountered truth, then I will give the cat to that person to keep. Otherwise, I'm cutting the cat in two and I'm giving half to each side just to stop this dispute."

The monks were shocked. They'd never heard of anything so horrible. Cutting the cat in two! I mean, they were in a peace monastery, for heck sake. How could this be?

They decided, okay, then. We're really good monks. We're really good meditators. Certainly, we can pass this test!

The most senior monk started. He comes in and he sits absolutely still with his eyes not moving. Because he thinks that's what meditation looks like.

The Master says. "Get out of here. That's not it." He sends him away.

Next comes in the strongest monk. He stands on his head and meditates. Certainly, that will do it… I mean, what could be harder than that, right? What could prove meditation more than standing on your head and meditating?

But the Master shooed him away saying, "That's not it."

Then three monks came in together. In three-part harmony they recited the most difficult prayer out of the holiest book of the Order. The Master sent them away saying, "No, that's not it."

One after the other, after the other, the monks came in and tried to prove their meditation. All of them failed. It went on all day. Finally, the master threw up his hands and said, "There's nothing to do. This place is a disaster."

He cut the cat in two and gave each side half of a dead cat.

Everyone was crying and weeping. They couldn't believe that such a horrible thing had happened. And on top of that, their whole lives had failed. They couldn't prove how spiritual they were. They couldn't prove that they were good meditators.

Just then. Rinjai, a young monk, comes back from the market. He'd been gone all day long. He comes back and everybody's crying and weeping. He asks, "What is going on?" And they told him the story.

He was aghast. He couldn't believe it. A thousand monks could not prevent one old man from killing a cat!

He marched right into the room, up to the master's chair. Slapped the master hard and shouted, "Don't you ever do anything that stupid again."

The master fell down on his knees in front of Rinjai bowing. He cried, "Finally! Finally, out of a thousand monks, all day long, here's someone who has proven their meditation. Someone who's proven that they know and understand truth. But you're too late. The Cat is already dead."

P.S. Don't worry about the cat. It's just a story. Do, however, worry about all the cats you create in your mind.

What is Real?

So, what's real and what's not?

In the story of Rinjai's Cat the master is asking all these monks to simply be able to show him that they know the difference between what's real and what's not real. That's what meditation and truth means. He's asking them to be able to show their meditation. Not to show how spiritually adept they are. And it's certainly not to show how deep in fantasy they are. It's to show if they're able to distinguish what's real and what's not real.

We are like a child playing.

Think about a child playing with her doll. The child playing with the doll is real. The game, whatever she's playing, it's a real game. But the fantasy, the little stories going in her brain, are not. She can take those and turn them into whatever she wants them to be.

How can you, inside your experience, find out what is real and what is not real?

So often our fantasies feel as real as the world. Our emotions feel very, very real. Even though, if you stop for a second and notice, they come and they go. Your thoughts? They come and go, and they come and go.

They do exist. They exist within the field of your thoughts. But it's not permanent.

Nonduality and Zen

Nonduality is good at teaching reality. It constantly takes everything and says, "No, it's not that. No, it's not that. No, it's not that."

Zen stories also do a good job of helping us with this, because it activates both sides of our brain. It activates the logical side and what we might want to call the mystical side at the same time.

So, what is real?

Proving Your Meditation

In the story of Rinjai's cat, killing the cat was really, really stupid. But the point of this story is that we have the same fantasies about spirituality today. We think spiritualty will look like something... and we also think the enlightened master would have to be perfect in all ways.

What Zen is saying is: Stop it. Stop looking for this crazy stuff. Stop trying to prove that you can meditate by standing on your head or how long you can meditate, or any crazy thing.

Today we have this crazy belief that if you're spiritual, you'll be prosperous. Some people use that as a criterion for themselves and for others.

So, this story is a challenge. Could you have passed the test? Could you have prevented the cat from being killed in this situation? How do you show your meditation and your understanding when in Zen (and in Nonduality too) what we're trying to achieve is ordinariness and simplicity?

Those are the things you can't show. It's like you can't on purpose relax. You can't force relaxation. Just like you can't force yourself to go to sleep if you're not falling asleep. Right?

So how do you show ordinariness besides in your everyday life? And how do we get away from all the false stories we've been told about enlightenment, awakening?

Where is this normality?

That's the strength of Zen. This story has now painted this picture in our heads of this monastery. It will always be in the vision of our mind. Are we being like Rinzai? Or are we being like all the monks who couldn't prove their meditation?

"If enlightenment looked like something... then everyone would try to look enlightened."

Death

A man once came to Sheik Faried and asked him, "What happens when we die?"

Faried just laughed. He looked at him and said, "You have come to the wrong person. I don't know anything about death because I'm alive. I'm not dead. I only know about life."

The purpose of Zen stories isn't to make us feel better. Or to make us feel we already know something. It's to shake us up. And that's our short story about death.

What Happens When You Die?

Now we have a Zen story about death. A hot topic. Yes?

Soooooo think… think about what happens when you die? What's your answer to that?

You probably had some sort of immediate answer. There's so many.

Some people will say, "Nothing it's just black. You go away and there is nothing.

Other people will say that you leave your body and float into this or that.

Some people will say you go to heaven, or you go to hell. There are all sorts of different ideas. I bet that you, reading this, had one of those many millions of ideas.

The Body

Probably you didn't think, or notice, that hey! Your body is dead! Laying there dead! You probably didn't even think about the body… even though that's the most obvious thing that has happened.

Why is that? Why isn't that the first thought that comes into your mind?

The Stories

The reason is that we have all, in some way, accepted the fact that the body will die. We've reconciled ourselves to the fact that the body will die.

All these other things that we create are stories around the fact that we accept the body dying. It justifies the fact that we know the body dies.

But notice how we don't have a huge issue about the fact that the body dies. We know what's going to happen to it as a matter of fact. Some of us have it planned. Someone will bury it, or you'll be cremated, or something like that.

We've accepted that as reality. As just part of life.

Think about that. The fact that you, on a fundamental level, have accepted the fact that the body will die.

The Certainty

Can we use that same certainty about the whole thing? There is as little to freak out about what happens to your soul, or what happens to your mind, as what happens to your body. There is no more reason to freak out about your soul than about the fact that the body dies.

It's all part of the same thing. It's already taken care of.

It's already taken care of, so what you think about it doesn't matter.

In our Zen story about death the master is saying, "Live your life. Don't ask me about death. I know about life."

Wherever the Wind Takes

A long time ago, in the land of Zen, there were two monasteries who couldn't get along. They were two different sects with different philosophies. They wouldn't talk to each other and couldn't agree.

There was a long-standing feud between these two 'religions.'

These two monasteries, they each had young boys in their employ, as young disciples. The boys would help the old monks with chores, and things like that.

Going to the Market

One of the jobs of the young boys was to go down to the market every day. Because of the rivalry of the two monasteries the boys were told, "Don't ever talk to each to each other. It's against the rules. Don't do it."

But boys will be boys, right? And so, they became curious. One boy, in particular, was very curious and as he was walking, he would peek out of his robe every time he passed the other young man.

One day he couldn't take it anymore, and so he stood at the side of the road and decided he was going to say something.

So. He stood there and very nicely said, "Where are you going?"

The other young boy stopped. Looked up and very philosophically said, "Wherever the wind may take."

What?

The first little boy was like... wait? What? That doesn't make any sense! He couldn't think of anything to reply back, at all. And he thought, "My masters were right. These people are weird. I have no idea what that meant."

The Lesson

He goes back home, and he confesses. He says, "I am sorry I disobeyed the rules. I see why you have these rules. Those people are weird. I asked the kid, 'Where are you going?' And he said, 'Wherever the wind may take.'"

The old master shook his head and said, "Yep. Yep. We knew that would happen. That's why we told you.

"But now the game is on, and we must win this battle!

"So, here's what you are going to do. Tomorrow, you go out on the road, and you wait for this young boy to come by. When he comes by you say, 'Where are you going?' and when he answers, 'Wherever the wind may take.' then you say to him, 'And what if the wind is not blowing?' And see what happens."

The boy was very anxious. He studied all night long. He wanted to make sure he got it right. This was one of the first lessons he had been given here at the monastery. He wanted to make sure he learned it right. He stayed up all night long, going over it in his head. To say, "And what if the wind isn't blowing? And what if the wind isn't blowing?"

By morning he was ready. He walked out to the crossroads and waited for the boy to come. Along comes the young boy from the other monastery. So, he looks at him and he says, "Where are you going?"

And the other boy replies. "Wherever the legs may take."

Now what???

Now it's legs!

His lesson was useless. He had no idea how to answer this. Again, the young boy dropped his head and ran back home defeated.

He said "I didn't know what to do. I was supposed to give the answer about the wind. But now he's talking about legs. And I don't know how to answer this."

Second Lesson

The master sighs and says, "Oh my Gosh. This is how those people always are. We have to beat them. So, here's what you do…

"You go back to the road. When he comes you ask him, and you say, 'Where are you going?' And if he says, "Wherever the legs may take' then you answer back 'And if you were born crippled? Then what?'

"Or if he says the thing about the wind, you reply with your bit about the wind. So, you've got two things. You are bound to succeed."

So again, the boy sat up all night long. Studying and worrying. Next day… he hadn't slept now for two days. He goes back to the crossroads. Here comes the other young man walking along. He's all ready. He looks at him and he says, "Where are you going?"

And the other boy looks at him and replies, "I'm going to the market to get some vegetables."

Now what?

This is exactly like studying religion. It's the way dogma is created. You can't ever get a right enough answer to meet up with life.

This Zen story is about pretending to look more enlightened than somebody else. And the craziness that comes from that.

We Try to Look Spiritual

So… yeah. Don't lie about it. We all try to look spiritual. Don't we?

We try to look more loving. We try to follow the books that we've read and look like we are supposed to look. We even have spiritual clothes.

We all do it! That is fabulous. You want to know what it means? It means we are human beings. We mimic. That's what we like to do.

There is even a saying "Fake it, till you make it." Maybe there is some value to that.

This week's Zen story shows these two different monasteries that are both trying to look more spiritual than the other — to the point where the older monks don't allow the younger monks, the boys that are working in the monastery, to ever meet each other.

Because they haven't learned the rules yet.

They might do it wrong.

They do meet. They do it wrong. That's you and me. That's the value of Zen stories. It gives us a laugh at ourselves. It puts a picture in our mind. Now you can see yourself doing it, or you can catch me doing it. Then you can have a little smile. Right?

Once you see yourself doing these things, then you see yourself. Now you have a choice in that moment. Are you going to continue doing it? Maybe you are good at it. Maybe there is some sort of famous spiritual teacher that you mimic who looks spiritual all the time.

Maybe you are like me… you don't hardly ever look spiritual ever.

That's the value of Zen stories.

What Does Nothing Look Like?

This week's Zen story, Where the Wind Takes is about nothing. It's two young boys who are meeting on the path. And the one boy is trying hard to follow the rules and look spiritual like his monastery. The other boy, is in the end, just going to the market.

You can't look like nothing. And this is so important to understand. If you've followed any of my teachings, if you've done any of the courses, on my website you'll know that nothing is actually what we are looking for.

It's not something you can look like. It's just living your life in an everyday manner. Go to the market when you are going to the market. It's like the last story when the prince was getting ready to shoot the vulture. He was doing nothing but shooting the vulture.

So that relaxed, simple, nothingness. That's what this story is about. What does that look like?

It doesn't look like anything. Or perhaps it looks like what you already are.

Never be For or Against

To hold the truth before you, never be for or against.

This is a fabulous Zen saying, but it's important to realize that this doesn't mean to not be discerning at all. What it means to constantly question the belief system that sits in your mind.

Always stop and examine yourself. Don't be for it. Don't be against it.

Where is the point in the middle where clarity can see what is going on in a particular situation? We like to judge things good or bad. But you want to hold the truth as nothingness itself.

If you can hold that firmly before you, then you will be willing to stop and watch yourself as your mind goes through the constant judgements of the day.

Bad Does Exist

If somebody does something horrible you can see the horribleness without clinging to the 'for it' or 'against it' bit. It's a way to live your life with constant examination about what's going on. With discrimination instead of belief.

The Fertility Blessing

This is a story about Bau Sin Tao.

One day he was sitting in the marketplace, with his disciples, and friends, and family all around. And a woman comes up to him. She says, "Bau Sin. Years ago, your master gave my mother a blessing and right after that she became pregnant with me and had me. I am now infertile, and I am wanting a child so bad. Would you please give me a blessing so that I can have a child."

Bin Tao looks at her and says, "Yes. Sit down with everyone else." And he gave blessings to everyone.

So, the woman went away. A couple of years. She still didn't get pregnant. After a while she'd had enough, and she came stomping back. She said, "You are a phony! My mother came to your master, and she got a blessing, and she was able to get pregnant. I came and got a blessing, and you didn't do anything for me! You're fake!"

Bin Tao looked at her, laughed and said, "But that's not how it works. Your mother didn't come asking for something specific. She just came to get a blessing. My master gave blessings to everyone all the time. Anyone who came would get a blessing.

"The fact that she got pregnant after that, and had you, was just an accident. It was just a coincidence. And I know. I was there when that happened."

She couldn't believe it. She still argued. "But your master. He was greater than you. He gave a blessing, and it did something. Your blessing didn't do anything at all."

But Bin Tau said "Your mother came not asking. Not demanding anything. You came demanding, so I thought 'Hey. What the heck. I'll give a blessing. It's a fifty-fifty chance. Maybe she'll get pregnant... then yay! It's me. I did a miracle. If she doesn't get pregnant, then hey. I know that nothing happened for her mother back then. So, I can get out of it.'"

> *Zen masters are very tricky folk. They are not going to necessarily do what you think they should do. They are not going to follow your rules.*

Rules for the Enlightenment Teacher

We have so many rules about what we want an enlightenment teacher to look like. What we want a spiritual teacher of any kind to look like. And there are lots of problems involved with that.

Number one, first and foremost is that you are going to miss the true teacher. Because as we've been learning through all our Zen stories, the actual teacher is very ordinary. They don't fulfill your miracles; they don't act the way you want them to act.

Asking to be Fooled

But more important than that, if you have all these rules about what you want a spiritual teacher to look like, then when you encounter someone who is very good at looking like your story… you are going to think they are the thing.

This is why we have such prolific numbers of fake spiritual teachers. We hand it to them!

All they gotta do is be a really good faker. All they gotta do is pull a couple of miracles out of their bag. These days it's even easier. The only thing they have do to be seen as a spiritual teacher is give somebody a good feeling.

The Zen Master

As we're learning in our Zen stories, the true Zen master does not necessarily make you feel good. Especially at the very beginning. That's why these Zen stories are so valuable. Because they paint a picture, in your mind of this world of awakening. They show how it follows very different rules than the rules we tend to set for our lives.

So keep listening to these stories. Follow these stories and let them paint a picture in your mind of something very different than what you may be expecting… in the teacher, and in yourself.

Stories and Myths

Human beings have been in a mental crisis for only a short period of time. We've been around as just-about-complete humans for millions of years. For 80,000 years we've been completely "DNA Us" with brains working exactly the way that our brains work today.

For most of that long, long time our brains fit in with the natural world. One of the reasons for that was our ability to tell stories, and to share knowledge through stories.

When we use stories as myth, what we today will call myth, they are actually "true." Because they work. What a myth does is paints a picture in our full mind. Both sides. What we, today, would call the left brain and the right brain, or all the different nodes of the brain.

These stories create pictures that help us live with each other, live with the world and understand the world.

Living in the Past and Future

An incredibly important function of the human brain is to to see patterns in the past and put them together to understand what's going to happen in the future.

Winter's going to come. We need to store up some food. Someone behaved badly… More than likely that person's going to behave badly again, unless we know to intervene. Day and night come regularly, and it's important to know.

So many aspects of being human is because of our ability to remember what happened in the past, put stories to it, and project that into the future. It's a totally good human thing to be able to do that.

It's handy to know where we went and where we are going.

When We Got Stuck

What we might call the beginning of our mental crisis was when our stories stopped matching up with our full mind. When we started making excuses for the things we didn't understand. We started believing un-useful stuff.

I don't know for sure, of course, but it seems that as civilization grew, we started using our stories to make us believe that we weren't part of the world. We became dominant minded and told stories that we were the dominant species, that we were the ones in charge of the world, that we were the bosses of everything.

That separation created madness. Then the madness, itself, started being in charge. When we started having wealth, and people being bosses of other people, it led to a state of confusion where what's going on inside of our brain is not useful our mental health.

How Mysticism Helps

Nonduality and Zen teachings are trying to take what has happened inside our imagination of who we are and turn it into something useful.

What Nonduality and Zen teachings are telling us is that we have a mental disease. Something is wrong with the way your brain works, so you can't trust any of it. You can't fix a broken mind with more broken mental concepts because you will always use these unhealthy stories and dreams to create meaning. The broken pieces don't fit together so the broken mind creates more and more complicated stories to explain it: dogma. Like our kids in the story, "Where the Wind Takes." On and on it goes getting more and more complicated.

Lies are Complicated.

It's like when you're telling a lie. You have to keep all your facts in line in order to continually support the lie. If you mess up, the people you're lying to are going to start figuring it out. In our mental crises today, our brains are full of lies.

Nonduality says: OK, so what do we do? What do we do about this?

It's the same question for Zen. This is what Buddha was looking for. He realized, "Something's wrong in my perception, what do I do about it?"

It seems frightening but the solution is actually very simple. What you need to do is bring yourself to a point of total zero. Realize, "My brain is not me. My mind is not me. These stories aren't me. I can't trust a single one of them."

You bring yourself down to complete zero, and when you get to the place where you know who you are as completely melded with existence, not identified with the mind not identified with the emotion, then that's day one. That's where you start being a full human being and can begin to piece it all together.

Perception from Zero

You've gone to zero and now you come back and can freely decide. Is it useful to love? Is honesty important? You can examine the stories from a place of freedom.

This is what scientists do. They basically say, OK, here's the world. We want to figure it out. We start with curiosity. Everything must be a theory to start out with, until it's proven. And then, as science got more and more complex, they started realizing that you can only prove very few things and everything else remains a probability. Which is really cool because it keeps you in a constantly curious state.

Are Myths Real?

So, stories and myths? Think of myths as stories that work within the context of how humans naturally live. But we are dealing with the modern mind, so we need to bring ourselves down to this point of zero, where we will allow ourselves to always go, "Everything's a theory. Nothing's fixed."

Don't be fixed on things. Then you can start looking at the old stories and decide: Are they useful or not?

Techniques for the Mind

Nonduality teachings and Zen stories are so good because they are a science to break through our damaged minds. What they do is take a little scenario and then twist it, the same way a joke ends. On a punchline. These techniques split our illusions apart.

Our Zen story about the fertility miracle is good this way. The Zen master does not behave at all like you expect he should behave.

He's supposed to make this miracle. He doesn't argue or get caught up in it, he creates a trick.

Taking the mind to zero doesn't have to be a big, huge, dramatic deal. Just accept the fact that all the things that are in our brain right now are not reliable. And it's not you. That's not you. It's just something that's been placed there by the stories we've been told since birth.

They are Just Stories

Like… you can read a book, Harry Potter. You read Harry Potter, right? That's just a story. You're not Harry Potter.

There are truths in it, but you are not Harry Potter. The book has wonderful wisdom about learning how to live, how to deal with life. But you're not the book. You can take the book; you can put it down. That's not you. It's just something that went into your brain. Before you read the book it wasn't there in your mind. After you read the book, it is there. Now you have this particular story in your head. It's not you. It is a tool that's been put in there. It's a story.

So, this is what we're trying to do with Zen. Erase the insanity by coming to the truth of who we are.

In a very simple way, we give it all up. We say it's all insanity. It's all nuts.

Who are you? Where is the you that's not nuts? That's what we are looking for. It's the part of you that doesn't need words. It's the part of you that decides which one of these stories you want to listen to. You are the master. The stories are not the master.

You've got to know who you are in order to step out of the madness and start becoming an agent. Unless you step completely out of it, you're going to always be spinning stories from your insanity.

Maybe we could say Zen is simply a way to become solid.

Your best opportunity to do this is when your mind is racing. You stop and say, "I am not my mind."

This is a healthy division. Now you've divided your experience into you and your mind. Now that it is seen as two, you can see that you are not it.

It's like, anytime you have that yakity yakity crazy thing going on in your head. Just say no. Stop. You're not that thought. You're not that decision. You don't have to understand it. Words will not help.

Ignore it as it chats away. You're not that. You're not that. You're not that.

Who are you? Find that out.

Zen says Don't Be Confused

Zen is simply saying that you don't have to be so confused. You can live your life in a simple way.

In our story about the Fertility Miracle, a woman comes, and she wants to get a miracle because she is infertile. Her mother had come to this spiritual master's teacher, and she ended up getting pregnant. So, this girl, from when she was very small, believed in miracles and believed that she existed because of a miracle.

This is a really good story. Don't discount the urgency of this situation. Way back in the land of Zen, being a mother was the only role that a woman had available to her. So, this was a serious thing.

When you don't know what to do about something. You are trapped in that situation. You are going to want a miracle.

This story is told in a lighthearted way, but in this situation it's not lighthearted for this person who is really wanting a miracle. Think about how this fits into your life. Today there are so many things that really are serious. What do you do?

Don't Be Confused

You need to know who you are and the simplicity of life underneath any seriousness so that you can deal with it.

What the story is saying is that the first so-called miracle that happened was just an accident anyway. The spiritual teacher knows that that is the case. The woman gets all upset about the fact that she wasn't able to have the same "miracle" but it doesn't change the reality of what's going on. The only thing that can change is the way that you can deal with it.

Whenever anything really bad happens you have two choices. One is that you can turn it into a wound. A giant wound, so that your whole life is consumed with this problem. This is very much what has happened to the woman in this story. It's a serious thing, but she's making it worse.

You can turn your problems into a wound. Or you can learn from it and become wise.

Again, I don't know the details of the society that she was living in, but almost always in human society there is a need for wise people. This woman was refusing to take the step to wisdom. Accept what is happening and become wise from it.

That's life. It's a hard thing. We don't always get what we want. We don't always get what we really need. So being awake and aware and turning everything that happens in your life into wisdom, is really our only choice.

We don't get to set the rules, do we?

THANKS

There is no worship
      and yet
without it your life is devoid
         of flavor.

Sing a mighty song of thanks
      to the wind that gives you breath
and the man who provides your anger.
      Both are a gift.

The Prince Remembers

A long time ago in the land of Zen there was a king. He only had one son and he was starting to get old. He started to be concerned that maybe his son was not ready yet to follow him as king.

So, as people did back then, he went to the biggest Monastery around and consulted with the master there. He asked, "How can I make sure that my son is ready to follow in my footsteps?"

The master gave him a very strange set of instructions. At first the King wasn't quite sure, but then he decided he'd better follow what the master instructed. So, the next morning the prince wakes up and there is the charioteer who says, "Come with me."

The charioteer puts the Prince in the Chariot, no clothes or anything, and drives him out of the Kingdom. He takes away the prince's crown. He takes away his robes. He gives him stinking old beggar robes, and hands him a beggar bowl, and says, "You have been expelled from the kingdom. Do not come back."

The prince freaked out he was crying, "What have I done? What did I do? I didn't do anything wrong?"

The charioteer said, "I don't know. They didn't tell me. All I was told was that I had to bring you here, dump you on the street and tell you to not come back or you'll be thrown in jail."

The Young Prince was devastated. He cried. He got really depressed, but after a while he got really hungry. He had no idea how to become a beggar, so he had to learn from the other beggars on the street. Slowly, slowly he learned how to be a beggar. He forgot completely that he'd ever been a prince. Begging became his whole existence.

Then one day he's standing on the street and suddenly, he hears the bells of the chariot. He wakes up and remembers, "Wait! What's that sound? I know that sound."

The charioteer comes driving up and says, "Wake up! You are the prince. Your father is dying and it's time for you to come home and lead the kingdom."

It took one second to remember. The prince immediately forgot that he was a beggar. He stood up. His chin lifted, and in that second, he transformed from beggar back into a Prince. Just because he remembered who he was.

> *This is exactly what waking up us like. This is why we call it remembering. You suddenly remember who you are, and the transformation is instant and complete.*

Mulla Nasrudine Coming or Going?

So Mulla Nasrudine met an old friend outside the door of his psychiatrist's office one day. She looked at him surprised, gave him a big old hug, and said, "Mulla, so long since I've seen you. We should get together sometime and have a cup of tea. But tell me are you coming or going?"

The Mulla looked at her and said, "Well. If I knew that. I wouldn't need a psychiatrist, would I?"

Tip Tip Tip Tip Tip

What's the Point of Mulla Nasrudine?

Osho loved to talk about Mulla Nasrudine because he is the perfect tool for a nothingness punchline. This story from the Osho Rajneesh archives and is obviously a modern story of Nasrudine. That's very interesting in itself because

Mulla is this character that has been used to tell stories for centuries. Maybe he was a real fellow at one time, but he is used as a fictional character for all sorts of stories now, to show us interesting aspects of ourselves.

This one is set in modern times and he's walking into the psychiatrist office. But that's not the point of it. Like all Mulla Nasrudine stories, and all Zen stories, the purpose is to bring us to that little point in our logical brains were stuff just doesn't make sense. It's the essence of a joke. It makes your brain stop for a second. You go… wait a minute? And get a little laugh.

That's the moment of nothing, that moment of zero that we are really looking for. Feel it and know it. That's the zero of awakening.

Be kind to your inner world. Zen doesn't mean being in a battle with yourself about what exists and what doesn't exist. It just means be fluid.

Taking Care of Your Mental Health

Mulla Nasrudine is a fun character to use for little snippets of wisdom. The story is obviously set in modern times and he's going to the psychiatrist. That's funny in itself because Mula Nasrudine, is this great Sheik, and here he is going to the psychiatrist. It makes us stop for a second and think that our mental health is our own responsibility.

One of the lies we've been told in our society is that whatever is going to happen in your mental health is just a given. It has nothing to do with your actual actions.

But in reality, it's more like a fluid flowing river. A river with rapids that you can master.

If you are searching for enlightenment, take care of yourself.

Here's something you've probably never thought about. Imagine, assume, that if you are searching for enlightenment, for awakening, for knowing who you are… Just assume that you will find it.

Then, think about it.

If that's the case, when you get there, when you find out who you are, when you were ready to take the first steps of being a fully awake, human being… Well, it would be great to be in good shape. Wouldn't it? It would be good to have your mental world, calm and peaceful. Yes? It would be good to have your body physically strong. It would be good to have your finances in good shape. It would be good to have your community healthy. To be well-known in your community and loved and appreciated. It would be good to have your family in good shape.

So do not neglect any of these things. If you are neglecting these things. If you are neglecting your mental health, or your community, it's because you don't really think you're going to get there. You're drifting in some unknown state trying to get to some other unknown state.

So no, take care of yourself.

Save Me from the Pillar

So, Sheik Farid was out teaching in the Square one afternoon. A man came who was full of questions. He was obviously very learned in Nonduality, and Zen, and Sufism. He asked, "How do I get rid of my concepts? How do I get rid of my mind? How do I free myself from all these things?"

Farid looked at him for a minute and then jumped up and ran over to a pillar. He grabbed onto the pillar, and he started shrieking and yelling. "Save me from the pillar! Save me from the pillar!"

The man, the seeker, was very shocked. It was a mess. People were running over, and it was a big, huge scene. So, he runs up to the Sheik and he says, "Farid! All you have to do is let go of the pillar. It's not holding onto you. It's not doing anything to you. Just let go of the pillar!"

Farid let go and said, "Exactly."

Letting Go

Remember that Aesop's Fable where the monkey stuck his hand down in the jar? He grabs something to eat, but then he can't pull his hand out because it's too big. Letting go is just like. Think of what it takes to… open your hand and let go.

The Pillar is not Holding You

The pillar is not holding you. That's obvious. But what we're talking about is stuff that's going on in your mind. Right? It feels real. So real.

Emotions feel very real… because they are. Emotions are actual chemicals shooting out of your brain in into your body. That's why you say you *feel* emotions. Because you *can* feel them.

Thoughts are what create emotions. In scientific reality your thoughts are real, your emotions are real. What spirituality is talking about, what Zen is talking about, what non-duality is talking about, is your attachment to these things. The only problem is being lost in the thoughts. Being lost in the emotions. It feels like something that is impossible to let go.

That's exactly what Sheik Farid is showing in our story today, "Save me from the pillar!" He's showing how we hold on to these things. They aren't holding on to you.

You can drop the attachment to things just like letting go of the pillar. Nothing will be hurt if you do it.

It's like forgiveness. You can forgive somebody without meaning that whatever they did was good. Forgiveness has nothing to do with them. Forgiveness is a choice you make in yourself.

Same with letting go You just let it go. Just like letting go of the pillar.

Is it really as easy as letting go?

Save me from the pillar is a great little story to have in your mind.

First of all… it's really easy to see it in other people. When somebody's going crazy about something it's easy to see and think, "Save me from the pillar!" When looking at someone else you can see how easy it would be for them to just drop it all. Right?

Hopefully you can apply it to yourself too when you're going crazy about something. What would it be like to just let it go? Is it really as easy as just letting it go?

The answer is yes and no. If letting go becomes a belief, now you're in total craziness. Now you have to let go of the belief of Letting Go. We all know how annoying it can be for someone to have that belief! Very often they're doing something awful to you, you get upset about it, and they just tell you to let it go!

When even this idea gets turned into a belief it gets turned into craziness.

But when you actually have something to let go, and *you* actually let it go… it's amazing. So, keep it simple. Keep it

61

relaxed. Be kind to yourself. Above all, always be questioning everything that's happening, and when you have that moment of let go that's a big Yahoo!

This Zen story is about letting go. But what exactly is it that you're letting go? It's not the thought. It's not the story itself, which may be true or may be kind of silly. But it's the clinging to the thought.

Atisha's Exercise

Let's try some experiments about how vast and pliable you are. This experiment is going to be a little backwards from what you're usually told to do in spirituality, but it's going to help you really explore yourself.

Start out by feeling your breath. Feel it gently as it pulls into your nose, how it touches you inside, and then it's released. Now imagine, as you breathe in, that you're breathing in all the pain and misery in the world. Hold it for a brief second and then as you breathe out breathe out all the love and joy in existence. Feel the transformation as you do it.

Breathe in all the misery. Transform it and breathe out all the love and joy.

So. All the pain and misery in the whole world can be changed in an instant inside you if you're concentrating on doing it. right? You just felt it. You just did it. You are an ordinary human being and can do this.

This means you don't have to run from bad vibes. There's no need to release pain and misery into the universe or try to get over it. Just that little bit of awareness while you were doing Atisha's exercise is enough to prove it.

You don't even have to have inner peace, complete 100 percent inner peace, in order to do this. You simply have to have the intention.

Your natural inner silence is the transforming force. There's no need to draw in good energy. You have the power and the Mastery inside yourself to transform it anytime.

Most of the time, in affirmation practices, we're told to avoid the bad, and get rid of it. You don't have to. You're strong enough to breathe it in and transform it yourself.

This is also an opportunity to bust another assumption. You assume that you're full of garbage right now, and all the good stuff is waiting to happen to you some other time. But this exercise proves that you can transform it yourself anytime you want.

Question Everything

We should question everything. When thinking about Atisha's exercise it is interesting because this exercise does the exact opposite of everything that we're being taught in the New Age world. We're taught that we must always think positive thoughts and never to think any negative thoughts. For if we do something terrible will happen.

Atisha's exercise is exactly the opposite. It is saying that you have the strength within yourself to transform things.

We breathe in all the misery of the world, and we bring breathe out happiness and love.

I'm not saying to avoid stuff either because Atisha's exercise teaches us how to be strong. If someone needs our assistance you don't want to internalize their pain. You need to be strong and able to help them.

Mostly it's showing us that we should question everything because we're surrounded by spiritual fads. People come up with all these beautiful teachings and "boom!" suddenly everybody is off on the new fad. We should at least question it. Look closely and see what every belief system turns into. The end result shows you it's quality.

Now question all the beliefs that you have accumulated through the past. How are those affecting your life?

This simple exercise can keep us from falling into the whole of craziness.

A Great Buddhist Teacher

When we're working with Atisha's exercise, we get the idea of what it's like to be with an authentic master. Atisha was a great Buddhist Master in medieval times. The simplicity of it is the anti-ego of it.

Breathe in all the pain and misery of the world and then breathe out love and compassion.

Typically, we see it the other way around. In our modern world we believe in create your own reality, and stuff like that. So many of the teachings we are given today is ego food.

But when you're working with a real master, they don't care how the broken part of yourself feels. They are only interested in bringing forth your mastery.

Atisha's exercise is very good at doing that.

As you play around with this exercise feel the difference between these two things. This is a fun way to do self-inquiry.

The Good Doctor

So Mulla Nasrudine is at the doctor. The doctor looks at him and says, "Mulla. It's not looking good. You are in bad shape. You don't have long to live. Have you written your will?"

Mulla looks at the doctor and says, "Oh yes. I have my will. I'm very wealthy and everything I own goes to the doctor who saves my life."

That's an infinite loop… right?

Stories about Mulla Nasrudine exist to make you go beyond your logical brain, where everything tries to make sense, and put that little "stop" to it… where you can see nothing.

Mulla's Inheritance
Nothingness

So Mulla Nasrudine finally sits down and writes his will, because to be in accordance with the law everybody needs to have a will. So, he sits down, and he writes it.

He wrote, "I have nothing. Let all the nothing that I have go to all my dependents." He listed them all out.

"Then," he said, "Anything left over goes to the poor."

How do you divide up nothing? You can't. There's nothing there. You divide it by anything and it's still nothing. That's the secret of Mulla Nasrudine's inheritance.

Mulla's Cards

So. Mulla Nasrudine was sitting and playing cards with his dog in the park.

A guy comes walking along and he watches him play. After a while he exclaims, "Mulla! Your dog is so smart. He's actually playing cards with you. I have never seen such a smart dog. Where did you get him? How did you train him?

Nasrudine looks at him and says, "What do you mean? He's not that smart. Every time he gets a good hand, he wags his tail.

Is the dog smart or is the dog dumb? Depends on your perspective... and that's what Mulla Nasrudine stories are always teaching.

Mulla and Nothing

These Mulla Nasrudine stories are about nothing. This is my favorite subject: nothing. If you really understand this, then you'll know how to look inside and find nothing.

Mulla has nothing and yet he's dividing nothing up between everybody else... and whatever's left over will go to the poor. That's quite ridiculous but it gives you a really good idea of the fact that nothing is nothing. This is the most important thing that you can realize in Zen.

If I told you right now to shut your eyes, look inside and see that you are nothing then you would turn nothing into a something. You would look inside and wait until that nothing happened, or try to look for a thing called nothing.

But how can you look for nothing?

Exactly the same. You don't own anything. How do you divide it between all your family? How do you leave the last little bit of nothing to the poor?

You can't. You can't divide nothing. Nothing is nothing.

The second you realize that nothing actually is nothing, and then you look inside yourself to see nothing, then illusion drops.

I am this.

It's like Eckhart Tolle talking about the power of now. Nothing and now are the same thing. Nothing happens in the now. If you are actually in "now' it's like nothing is happening.

So, nothing is the key.

Stories about Mulla Nasrudine are to make you go beyond your logical brain, where everything tries to make sense, and put that little "stop" to it... where you can see nothing.

Mulla's Ticket

So Mulla Nasrudine was boarding the train, getting ready to go on a trip. He jumps on and meets the ticket taker who says. "Mulla. I need your ticket."

Mulla starts looking everywhere. He looks in his hands. He looks in his pant pockets. It's not there. He throws down his bags, and rips open all his luggage. He pulls everything out, going through bag after bag.

It's this giant disaster. The line is piling up behind him. Everybody's getting very annoyed and Mulla keeps crying, "Where's my ticket? Where's my ticket?"

Finally, the Ticketmaster, exasperated, says "Mulla! Why don't you look in your left-hand jacket pocket? That's where almost everybody keeps their ticket. You haven't looked there yet."

Mulla looks at him, shocked, and says, "But if I look there, and it's not there, then all hope is lost."

In this story Mulla is afraid to look in the most logical spot for his train ticket... because if it's not there all hope is lost. This is showing us one of the ways we undo ourselves. We are afraid of looking for ourself in the most obvious spot. We look everywhere for spirituality except for where it resides.

Saint Francis said, "What you are looking for is where you are looking from."

Talking About Mulla's Ticket

This is such a telling tale about how most of us conduct our spiritual searches. We are searching everywhere except for the place of "I am."

Mulla's ticket is one of my favorite Mulla Nasrudine stories because we are searching everywhere, searching everywhere.

We even have sayings like: it doesn't matter what path you're on... they all lead to the same place.

Nah. No. Most paths lead into a maze. It's like Mulla searching in his luggage and throwing his clothes all over the train. He's making this big mess. Most paths, most leaders, literally take you away from yourself. You're looking and looking for yourself everywhere but in yourself.

Just look with yourself and you'll find yourself.

But... you're like, "No. If I look there and I'm not there, then All Is Lost."

Literally that's the point of everything. If you look at yourself, with yourself, with who you actually are, what will you find? You're gonna find out that you're not that big of a deal. There's nothing. There's nothing about you that is separate from everything... and that is the moment of Awakening.

All the searching and searching and searching and searching is literally just trying to avoid that moment of accepting yourself. So, this is the best story to keep in your mind.

Yes, it's a funny story. The image of Mulla looking and looking and throwing his shirts around. It's fixed in your brain now. Every time you're sitting around with your friends and talking about the path, talking about spirituality, this image will be there. Or you're sitting with yourself, or you're meditating, you'll keep seeing Mulla.

Keep in mind that, more than likely, the ticket is in your left-hand breast pocket.

You are you, nothing else.

The Blue Lotus Flower

Once Upon a Time. Back in the day of Buddha, when Buddha was alive on the planet with us, there was a simple man. He was a shoemaker, and he had a pond behind his house. One day he goes out, it's not in season, but a beautiful blue lotus flower bloomed.

The man thought, "Oh this will make such a wonderful offering for the Buddha!"

He picks the flower, and he goes out onto the road where people were passing by to go see Buddha. A very rich man comes along, and the rich man sees the blue lotus flower and he says, "Oh! What a beautiful lotus flower! I want to buy it and give it to the Buddha. How much do you want?"

The Shoemaker was a simple man. He said, "I don't know how much. You make an offer."

The rich man says. "I'll give you a hundred rupees for it."

The shoemaker was blown away. He couldn't believe it could be worth that much! He was just about to hand it over when up comes a king. The king sees the blue lotus flower and he says, "I'll give you 200 rupees for that blue lotus flower. It's so gorgeous I must be the one that gives it to Buddha."

So, the man, of course, sells it to the king. Because who's going to argue with the King anyway?

The King takes the lotus flower, and he goes to see Buddha. Of course, you know, he goes right in. He gets right up to the front of the line... because well, privilege, power yeah. So, he goes up and he sees Buddha and he hands him the blue lotus flower. He's so proud of this gift that he had brought!

Buddha looks at him and says, "Drop it."

The king is just amazed. But he does what he's told. He drops the blue lotus flower.

Buddha looks at him again and says, "Drop it!"

And the King's like... what do you mean? How crazy are you? I just dropped it!

Buddha looks at him again and says, "Drop it."

Of course, he wasn't talking about the blue lotus flower at all. He was talking about this tremendous ego and all the greed that had been behind this bringing of the blue lotus flower.

Walk on the Water

So, a man came up to Ramakrishna. He was standing by the river and the guy says, "I can walk across the water on that River."

Ramakrishna looked at him and said, "Wow. Really that is amazing. How long did it take you to learn how to do that?"

The guy answers with great spiritual airs, "Of course, because I am so spiritually advanced it only took me 18 years to learn."

Ramakrishna looks at him and says, "Eighteen years! What a waste. For two rupee I can get across that river on the ferry in 10 minutes."

Sunrise Zen

Okay… so there was this non-duality teacher. He's sitting out on the deck, the veranda, of the ashram with all his students. Watching the sunrise.

He looks at it and asks, "If the world was flat, and the sun revolved around the earth, what would the sunrise look like?"

The students are surprised and don't know what to say…

He answers. "It would look just like this."

Then he asks, "If the world was round. If it was revolving and moving around the Sun. What would the sunrise look like?"

He answered his own question, "It would look like this."

Believing that a thing is so doesn't make it so.

This is a perfect story about how our perceptions are often the thing we pay attention to, when it's reality that matters. Perceptions are only a tool. In fact, you can manage them. They shouldn't manage you. If you take your perceptions down to the point where you can see yourself interpreting the world with past conditionings, down to the point of zero, and face life with complete curiosity then you can start to see seeds of the truth.

When I look at a sunrise or a sunset, I know so much about it scientifically. I know about air and clouds and how colors are made. But it's the part of me that has no words at all that enjoys it.

Sunrise Teaching

Our Sunrise teaching is such a great teaching because it blends science and Zen. Knowing how the world works helps us use our minds and, as a result, see how our minds work.

Like, how does the wind blow and turn into electricity? We know bits about that. Engineers and scientists know all the details about it. The rest of us? We don't really need to know every single bit of it, but it helps put our world together to know how things work.

When I have an understanding about the world, I worry about it less. If we worry about it less, then we stop making up stories.

It's also interesting to know that there are people who know the answers to things that I have no clue about. It stays a wonderful mystery to me and if I'm smart, I ask them when I want to know something.

There is no need to cling to believing the world is flat when new information comes along. The sunset stays the same when you know the truth.

Z is about becoming one who knows that you don't need to know everything, and you don't always need words to understand things. It's also about knowing that there is a truth, and we can move towards it. Then we can stop grasping.

This Too Shall Pass

Once there was a great king. He came to a Sufi Mystic and he asked for something. He said, "I'm trying to conquer great lands. Could you give me a Talisman, or a saying, or a mantra or something that will help me?"

The Sufi Mystic looked at him and smiled, in the way that Sufi Mystics do, and took a ring off his finger. He gave it to the king, and he said there's only one demand I have of you. You cannot open the ring and see what's inside until all is lost, until literally nothing can be done for whatever situation you are in."

The king thought, "Well... I mean, how much help is that going to be?" But he took it anyway. He went and he had great battles and conquered many lands and then his fortunes turned bad. All his battles were lost, and he was running by himself. He was being chased by a whole army. He runs, and he runs, and he runs up a mountain and down a ravine. And he can hear the horses coming and he knows that all is lost. He suddenly remembers the ring. He looks down and opens the ring, and there was a saying inside. It said, "This too shall pass."

He paused, and as he was pausing the entire army ran past the little hiding place that he was in, and he was saved.

After that this mantra became his meditation. "This too shall pass."

And he became a wise and compassionate leader because he realized this is the case for everyone else too not just for him.

This too shall pass.

The Good and the Bad

This Zen story is great because it's two different things. It's totally bull and it's also a very wise important point.

It's total bull because, I mean, come on! In this story everything's lost and then he looks at the ring and boom! Magically he's saved. So, you know what our greedy spiritual minds are going to do with that right? We're going to start believing that there is a magic pot, or a potion we can use to make everything always come out right. If we always just believe "This too shall pass" then we'll magically drift through life and end up with everything we want.

Aaaaand.. we'll all want to nod wisely and tell others all about this. All the time... yes?

But that's not what this story really means.

If we go deeper. If we can get past the magical thinking, we can start seeing what's really important about this story.

First of all, the Mystic gave the saying to the king in a way that it would not become a belief system. He was told to not open the ring until things are really, really bad. Imagine if the king had cheated and he'd opened it up and he saw that it said, "This too shall pass?" He would have just turned it into a pedantic saying. "This too shall pass." And he would have become one of those annoying people who are always telling everybody their beliefs.

But he didn't. He had to be at the point where he could really learn the lesson before seeing the message. That's the true magic of this story. It shows the difference between believing and knowing.

So don't turn "This too shall pass" into a saying for you. We're all annoying enough anyway. Right? Don't add this fuel to your mix.

The important spiritual insight of this story is that experience is greater than knowing.

And finally, the real question is… who is the experiencer?

Is There a God?

Buddha was teaching one day. People were gathered all around, and people would come up one by one and ask questions. A man comes up and asks. "Is there a God?"

Buddha looked at him for a moment and said, "No. there isn't a god."

More people came. After a while another man shows up. He walks up and he says, "Is there a God?"

Buddha looks at the man for a moment and says, "Yes there is a God."

Now Ananda was standing by and he's like… wait? What? I'm trying to figure this out? He answered one thing one way, and then he answered the same question another way. What's the actual answer?

Buddha kept on teaching and towards the end of the afternoon another man came up and he asked, "Is there a god? Some people say there is, and some people say there isn't, and I can't quite sort it together."

Buddha looked at this man and then he just closed his eyes. It was a beautiful afternoon. Birds were singing and you could hear the river going by. Buddha sat there for about an hour with his eyes closed in this manner. The man also closed his eyes, listened to the birds and listened to the water. After about an hour they both opened their eyes together and the man said thank you. "Thank you for the answer," and he left.

Now Ananda was really perplexed, and he finally asked, "But what's the answer? To the first guy you said one thing. To the second guy you said another thing. With the third guy you didn't say a single thing!"

Buddha looked at him and answered that the first man was convinced that there was a God. Buddha could see that and so, in order to shake up his belief systems, he said no there isn't a god. The second man was an atheist, and he was convinced that there was no God at all. So, Buddha answered him the opposite. The third man was actually questioning. So, Buddha just sat silently and let him discover it on his own.

Mulla's Big Stick

So. Mulla Nasrudine is out on a hike with all his friends. He has this big, huge, tall walking stick. He's struggling along, trying to get up the hill with this big, huge stick.

Finally, one of his friends says, "Mulla. You know. If you just cut the bottom off that stick, a foot or so, it would fit you a whole lot better. It would work a whole lot better."

Mulla looks at him and says, "Oh you fool! The bottom of the stick isn't the problem! Why cut that off! The problem is this end up here, at the top!"

Thinking about Mulla's Stick

Mulla Nasrudine stories, and so many Zen stories, are fun because they twist the mind. Right? They show that all the thoughts that go in our mind can't completely grasp reality. It's a brain teaser.

The top of the stick is way up high. If you cut off the bottom of the stick the top of the stick will come down, right? Or conversely, cut off the top it will also be shorter, the right size.

The story itself is so silly but it shows how our fixated minds can also be so silly. AND it shows that we are able to see this disconnect. You can see it instantly!

You got the joke, right?

And that shows that you are capable of "getting" that moment of awakening. You're smart enough to figure it out. You are the who can see that the words in this story are ridiculous!

You are that.

Bodhidharma's Student

Bodhidharma became enlightened in India, and he wanted to teach. He wanted to show people what he had found in this new way to live that would transform life, but he couldn't find anyone who would listen to him.

Finally, he goes to China thinking he might find someone there. He goes there. A long way. It's not much better. Nobody is really interested in Enlightenment. They're only interested in power stories or pretending that they already know.

He finally throws up his hands, goes into a cave and just sits there staring at the wall. He says, "I will not turn around until I find someone worthy to teach."

He sat there for years turning away everyone who came in. Refusing to turn away from the wall.

Finally, a man comes in, sits down behind him and just sits there silently for hours. Bodhidharma does not turn around. At last, the man stands up. With his sharp knife and one quick sweep he slices off his hand and shouts, "Turn around and teach me or the next thing I'll do is slice off my head!"

Bodhidharma knew he had found the right student.

Bodhidharma and Trust

Our Bodhidharma story is pretty harsh. Bodhidharma is looking for a student. I don't know if it's true. It's a story that Osho told. So, who knows?

But this is an important story for several reasons. It's shocking and so we remember it. The picture of that guy standing there with his hand cut off sticks in the mind! Also, it speaks a lot about the search for enlightenment. It's not a game. You need to be really serious about making significant changes in your consciousness.

At the beginning especially it's not going to make you feel better. If you're only looking to feel better, you would do better to watch a good movie. Or buy a workshop that you can find out in the spiritual marketplace.

On the other hand (pun intended), if you want to really find enlightenment you need to have a commitment to it. In the beginning you are trying to use the ego to slice off the ego. It's a tricky business!

In this story the guy slices off his hand, right? Then he says – next I'm going to slice off my head!

Would you be willing to slice off your hand for something that you didn't think you could achieve? He must have been so certain of himself. He was certain that if

Bodhidharma would just turn around that he would find transformation.

Another interesting point of the story is: here's Bodhidharma, you know, one of the best spiritual teachers in history. And yet he couldn't find anyone in India to teach. In that vast spiritual country, there was no one capable of paying attention. Everyone ignored him there. He had to go all the way to China.

The story is gory, yes, but these are two really really important takeaways. First of all, there are enlightened people all over the place and they are looking for you. They are looking to teach you. Don't be a person who can't see.

Secondly, have dedication and a huge trust in your own ability. Be willing to slice off your hand and you'll be willing to let the ego drop.

Words and Prayer

I've been running across a lot of Native American stories lately that show an advanced understanding of living in the non-dual Zen state.

I'm not going to tell the story myself because you can hear it directly from a Navajo Elder.

Search YouTube for: The Truth About Prayer... A Native American (Navajo) Perspective.

This story is deeply interesting because it's talking about one of their creation stories. They have the Holy people who are organizing the world. He is very specific to say that they're not creating the world, because you can't create anything out of nothing (very nondual, yes?). So, they were organizing the world and they did it with words. Words are powerful.

The Holy People allowed the five-fingered beings (humans), to have words and the people started abusing the power that the words gave them. So, the holy people were going to take words away from the people.

The people wanted to keep the words. They went through a whole process journeying to the holy people. Finally, it was agreed that human beings, the five-fingered beings, could keep words if they prayed and if they prayed properly.

What's so interesting about this is that in non-dual teachings what we're talking about is words. We are trying to deal with the fact that the language in our minds goes wrong. We get addicted to the language in our heads and we start thinking that we're separate. And then, because human beings are so powerful when we work together, we're able to create too much. Out of that creation can come destruction.

Out of that creation *has* come destruction.

In this story the Holy People have said that the way to deal with this mind, with these words, with the way that we get addicted to words in our minds, is to pray. And to offer a prayer, like you are giving something of value. That's fascinating because when we pray, we are using words. But when the prayer is an offering, the words seem to access a different side of our consciousness. This enhances the side of us that doesn't put words together and turn them into destruction.

So, watch this story. Hopefully you can see how this kind of teaching, this way of pointing at the words, is a way to bring the human brain into balance. A balance between the side of us that sees words, knows words, uses words, gets addicted to words, and the side of us that is just silent and knowing. Both of these sides are extremely important to be human beings.

And we should pray and pray properly.

Offering a Prayer

So why would prayer help us with our addiction to words?

The addiction is manifested in the way that words get stuck in our head. It's the way they suck away our consciousness and make us think that we *are* words. How could prayer help with that?

In this native story, when the elder is talking about prayer, he's talking about something very specific. He's not talking about the kind of prayer where you're praying to Jesus and asking for stuff. He's not talking about chanting and trying to go into a bliss state through chanting. He says that Navajo prayers are teachings. They're stories with lessons. Stories that are teaching us how to be decent human beings.

East and West

In eastern traditions we are given the technique of meditation. In the context of eastern teachings meditation is helpful because what you're trying to do is get underneath the words. The same words we are hearing about in this native story.

Many people find meditation hard. It looks easy from the outside, but most people can't sit down and just go "Pow!" It doesn't happen easily by itself. Sometimes you sit down, and your mind goes crazier than it's ever been. It's worse when you are meditating in order to achieve something.

Again, on the other hand, prayer is a sacrifice. It's something you give. It calms the greedy mind simply by the act of giving.

One interesting thing in this story is that Wally talks about how he really loves a few particular Christian prayers because they are structured like good prayers. One of them is the Our Father. What's interesting about this is that the Our Father prayer does give a little story. It's a morality saying, and it's also not your regular words. In the Catholic tradition you give it as an offering, a sacrifice.

Prayers like these are offered up. You offer it as a prayer. It's a thing, a real thing that you can give.

In the Our Father you're not really asking for anything, you are *giving* a prayer.

Try adding that into your meditation: Our Father who art in heaven, hallowed be thy name, thy kingdom come, thy will be done, on earth as it is in heaven. Give us this day our daily bread and forgive us our trespasses as we forgive those who trespass against us. Amen.

Say it like a prayer. A simple prayer and nothing more. It doesn't need to have a special meaning.

Go ahead and do it in English. Just the regular version that you know, because it of comes off your tongue easily and you can simply offer it as a prayer.

The part of our brain that tries to understand everything with words, and put names on things, is really the smallest part. The vast majority of our Consciousness is a silence with no words.

Temporary Joy

I'd like to offer another great non-duality teaching from a Navajo Elder. Again, I pass you to his video on YouTube so you can hear it in his words.

Search YouTube for: About The Evil One: Native American (Navajo) Teachings.

He is talking about evil, and evil beings who come. What happens is they fool us. And one of the ways that they fool us is by giving us temporary happiness. Happiness that comes and goes. Confidence that comes and goes. Joy that comes and goes.

Zen teachings are very similar. I've never heard anyone call temporary joy evil, but that's a poignant way to look at it.

In Zen we are talking about a ground of being that is a permanent state. It's a ground that you can be standing in at all times. It doesn't falter.

The easiest way to describe it is that it is knowing who you are. It is something so simple and obvious that you can't ever unsee it. Knowing that you're nothing, and everything. When you're standing always in this solid awakened state you're not buffeted back and forth. It's not temporary.

So, it's very interesting that Navajo teachings have this same description. Wally describes it fabulously in the video because what happens is when you have only impermanent happiness, then you end up throwing a fit and causing problems. You cause destruction.

Why?

Because happiness feels good. We like it, right? It's wonderful. Then, when it goes away, we feel broken and miserable. We want it back. We'll do anything to get it back.

Same with confidence. When confidence goes away, we feel broken, and we want it back. We'll do crazy things to try and get it back! I mean... that's almost the definition of a sociopath. Right? Somebody who's willing to do crazy, insane things just to have a fleeting moment of happiness and power.

In Zen teachings we say it's possible to have a permanent, solid happiness. We're not talking about a drunken happiness, dancing all the time. We're talking a deep inner joy. It almost couldn't be called joy. It almost couldn't be called happiness, because it's more like a hum of ordinariness. It's more like something that holds you up all the time.

So, if your experience is of fleeting happiness, fleeting confidence, that means it comes and it goes. Don't get fooled by this temporary happiness, it's not going to get you anything. Know that there is something deeper down. Keep up your meditation, and your work to discover your mind for the fool that it is. Don't let it fool you. Find out who you are underneath it: nothing.

There is actually nothing in your mind. If you close your eyes and simply look inside... really, honestly look. You'll see nothing. Take a moment and peek. There's nothing there. Only absolute silence. It's the silence of the universe. Feel that. Step into that. That's where this solid confidence, the solid hum of existence that you are, lives. It's what you are looking from.

You are Not Temporary Joy

This Navajo teaching is fascinating because it's exploring this idea of temporary joy, temporary confidence, and how these things mess up the human mind.

Why? Why not? Why not get happiness when you can? Why not get confidence when you can?

It's because when it's not real, then it's fake! It comes and it goes, and when it goes away then you're left longing for the happiness. It's like a drug.

People who go to retreats experience this a lot. You go to the retreat. You have this fabulous time, and then you come home, and you slip back into your regular life. You slip back into whatever level of misery it might be. The temporary joy is gone.

Consumerism (which is destroying the planet) is all about temporary joy and temporary satisfaction. It never works. In the end you cannot buy enough things to make you happy. You can't buy enough things to give you a satisfied life.

So why is this warning about temporary joy given in the Navajo teachings?

Of course, I don't know. I can only speculate, but it seems that it must be because they are a wise and long-lasting civilization. In their deep history they discovered what brings on full community joy. They discovered what works for everybody. The only thing that can work is a lasting, abiding, solid being of your authentic self.

Joy that comes and goes creates narcissism, and that's how you break communities.

We Have Our Own Solutions

Non-duality teachings are about identifying temporary things. It means "Not two." So, it's literally an exercise in discovering what you aren't. How to find what is not real. Nisargadatta perfected the practice. Find out, first, what you are not and then you can start getting an idea of what you are.

What you are looking for is where you are looking from.

It turns out that you are not anything at all... so it becomes a very, very simple practice. "I'm not this. I'm not that. I'm not this. I'm not that." Until everything is gone, and nothing is revealed to be you looking.

Love: Emotion or Action?

Another good teaching from our Navajo Elder this week about love.

Search Youtube for: Family First: Navajo Love through Sacrifice. The Traditional Way

He talks about the difference between what he hears from English society, how we view love, as compared to what he was taught in the Navajo traditional teachings.

We see love as an emotion. "I'm feeling that I love you." We experience it as an emotion. It's a wonderful emotion. It feels so good to love! We *love* to feel love.

Love feels really good. In fact, it's almost like a drug. We want to have more and more and more of this feeling.

In the Navajo tradition love is not an emotion it's an action. It's things that you do. It's the way you take care of your family. It's your responsibilities. It's sacrifice. It is what you do as a human being, as a decent human adult. It's the way you take care of people around you.

This is this is very different than love as a feeling.

This is also close to what Zen teaches because Zen teaches that emotions are fleeting: they come and they go, they come and they go. Although they are real, they are not you. They don't define you.

When you find the ground of being, the solidness that is you, then you are a fully functioning adult human being. When you find that quality, solid in yourself, then emotions can come and go without really swaying you. Then you get to choose.

You don't really get to choose your emotions because emotions kind of just come up. Usually something triggers them. You do, however, get to choose how you enhance them, and the actions that you take to create them. But the emotions themselves come and go.

You also get to choose to not be attached to them.

This is similar in Zen and Navajo teachings. Navajo teachings say love is an action. It is the things you do. And then, if you do all these things that take care of your family what ends up happening, the end result, is the *feeling* of love.

You do something very loving for somebody, you do an action, and then the result may be the feeling of love. It's the result, not the thing itself.

I like this idea of focusing on the action rather than the brief fleeting emotion.

Love is an action.

Ten Friends Counting

Okay… so there were these ten friends. Way back in the land of Zen, a long time ago, before cars or anything like that. They decided to go on a journey. So, they got everything they needed and off they went.

They are walking along, and they come up to this big river. The only way to get across was to swim, so they all jump in and swim across to the other side. They gather together on the other side and start to get ready to get going again.

One of them says, "You know. We should probably make sure that everyone made it across."

Everyone agrees. "Yeah. Really good idea. Let's count ourselves."

So, they got in a circle and the one guy started counting everybody in the circle. He starts with the guy to his left. "One, two, three, four, five, six, seven, eight." And ends with the guy to his right. "nine."

He gasps, "Oh my gosh! one person is missing! There are only nine!"

His friend standing next to him says, "It doesn't look like anybody's missing. You must have done it wrong. Let me do it." So, he starts counting starting with the guy next to him and goes around the circle. "One, two, three, four, five, six, seven, eight, nine."

Then he exclaims, "Oh no! Someone's missing!"

They all start crying. "Who is it? Our friend is missing. Probably drowned in the river."

Then a Zen monk comes walking up. He asks, "What's the problem."

They sob, "Our friend died crossing the river and we're so upset. When we started out there were ten of us, and now there are only nine." The monk looks at him and says, "What? Are you sure."

They showed him how they were counting around the circle.

The monk says, "Let's start again." He counts around the circle. "One, two, three, four, five, six, seven, eight, nine," Then without stopping the monk takes his finger and pushes it against that first fellow's chest. "Ten. Look you're all here."

The man had forgotten to count himself.

You are You

Every one of these Zen stories point exactly to what we're talking about in enlightenment teachings. You are trying to find yourself. The question is, "Who are you?"

This story points directly at it (pun intended.)

In this week's story it's glaringly obvious. The ten friends are in a circle counting themselves. They start around: one, two, three, four, five, six, seven, eight, nine… Oh no! Someone's missing.

Who is missing is the guy counting. He forgets to count himself because he can't see himself.

Enlightenment, in a nutshell, is when you see yourself. More specifically… when you realize where you are looking from.

Now picture that you are standing there in the circle. You are looking outward. Imagine yourself looking out at your ten friends in the circle. You see everyone but yourself.

That's how we live life. It's so easy to miss counting yourself. This sounds like a stupidly ridiculous story… because it is. How do we miss something so blazingly obvious! You are you. You don't have to hold out for some magical mysterious, wonderful bliss filled thing… you ARE the one looking out at the circle.

One, two, three, four, five, six, seven, eight, nine… ten. You.

That's it.

Rabia's Needle

So, one day Rabia was out in the Village Square. She was on her hands and knees, crawling around, gasping and crying. "Oh no! I've lost it! I've lost it!"

All the village people came running to help. Obviously, she was in such distress. They asked, "Rabia what's wrong?"

Rabia said, "I've lost my needle. I can't find it. It's got to be here somewhere."

All the people started crawling around in the in the dirt, trying to help. Digging around and looking for the needle. Finally, one of the wiser women in the village asked, "Rabia. Where exactly did you drop it? If you could tell us where you dropped it then we could look there, and we'd probably find it faster."

Rabia replied, "Oh, I dropped it in my hut."

The woman was exasperated and said, "We'll never find it here if you dropped it in your hut. Why are we looking here?"

Rabia replied, "Well. It's dark in my hut."

Look Where It Is

Rabia was a mystic in the 1st century. All these years later we really aren't any different. Rabia was trying to show the people in the village that you must look for a thing where it is. You're not going to find it looking for it where it's not.

That's exactly what Zen and Nonduality are telling us. That's why we go through this whole process of, "Not two. Not two." It's why Zen always ends with a pinch. Looking for all the things we are not.

You are not things outside of yourself. You are not the thing that you're looking at. Mysticism is you. That's where you'll find it. But that's where we don't want to look because we think that it's dark inside.

In actuality, there's nothing inside you that's separate from anything that's outside of you. There's literally no separation. There is no darkness in there. But we must go over it, and go over it, until finally we're able to realize it. See it. Find it. Know it.

So, at the very least… start looking in your Hut. That's where you dropped your needle. You will find yourself in yourself.

More accurately, you are not *in* there. You are that

Three Blind Men

There were three blind men and they come upon an elephant. They were trying to figure out what it was. What is this thing?

Each of them examined a different part of the elephant.

One was feeling its legs and says, "Oh my gosh! It's huge. It's massive. It has hard, tough skin."

Another one was feeling its tail and says, "No. It's not really all that big. It's kind of skinny. I can get my hand all the way around it. It's hairy here at the end."

The third one was feeling its trunk and says, "No. No. You guys are wrong. It's very wiggly, and it kind of snorts here at one end."

None of them were able to see the full elephant and so they each got only the one small part. This is exactly the way we're all approaching spirituality because we each just see just one small part and fixate on it.

Confused About Elephants

The elephant story shows how easy it is for us to get confused if we don't see the big picture. Especially since the big picture is really big. This speaks to our entire society too. If nobody sees the entire picture then it's hard to know what an elephant is, to know what reality is, or to even to know what life is.

This is why the spiritual search gets so messed up. Especially when there's so many spiritual teachers who are teaching a small part of it. Each one teaching the tiny part that they can see with their limited vision. That's why some people are teaching create your own reality, and some people are teaching meditation, and some people are teaching chanting. It's because they don't see the full picture.

Sadly, they are as confused as you are. Probably even more confused.

It's also true that an awakened teacher can only teach a small part of reality because the people that the teacher is talking to are only able to grasp small parts. It takes a broad vision to see the whole picture at the same time. To really grasp the entire elephant you gotta become unblind.

Elephants and Science

The elephant story shows why the scientific method is such a great way to examine life. It's a powerful way to examine reality because the scientific method insures you never

106

have the opinion of one person becoming "the truth." Everything is always up for argument. Everything grows on what came before it.

Sometimes the opinion of one scientist, or a group, can become "the truth" for a little while. But eventually somebody will challenge it. In the end it's never fixed.

Even more exciting is the fact that the scientific method is a way to get a large number of brains working together. Over time, and over space. All around the world. This makes it possible to get the biggest picture possible.

One thing that's really cool about scientists is that they are super competitive so they're always trying to show each other up. Every idea is subject to challenge so only the best and most proven ideas make it through. That's a great way to approach things because it means we are always questioning and always approaching life with curiosity.

It would be wonderful if we also did that for spirituality. We should always be arguing with each other about what's true, about what's helpful. Rather than arguing about whether or not we are pure enough.

All About Monkeys

So, a man comes to a spiritual teacher and says, "Show me enlightenment." This was back in the time in the days of Zen. The teacher looks at him and says, "Oh it's easy. You just go home, for one night. You spend the entire night not thinking about monkeys and come and report to me in the morning."

Of course, the guy comes back in the morning, and you can guess what happened. He's bleary-eyed. He hasn't slept the whole night. He says, "Oh my gosh! all I could do was think about monkeys all night long!"

And the master says, "Okay now are you willing to put some time into this? Learning how to master your mind and to find out who you are not a simple fix.

The guy bows and says yes. He, at least, saw how difficult the path is going to be.

Look Who's Nothing

Mulla Nasrudine was a saintly and pious man. He went one day to the mosque and went inside pray. He goes up to the front. He kneels down and prays with great reverence, "Oh Holy One. I am nothing next to you. I am nothing, and I offer you this prayer."

Then he hears a sound. So, he jumps up and goes and hides behind the curtain.

In comes a magnificent Sheik. He has a huge hat and beautiful robes. He goes up, and kneels down and says, "Oh Allah! I am nothing! I am nothing next to you. Thank you for accepting my prayer." He hears a noise, and he jumps up and hides behind the curtain.

In comes the lowliest beggar from off the street: dirty, skinny, uneducated. He comes up to the front and kneels down. He starts praying, "I am nothing. The only thing I have to offer is this prayer."

Back behind the curtain, Mulla looks at the Sheik and sneers, "Ha! Look who thinks he's nothing!"

Competition and Power

So many Zen stories are trying to warn us that spirituality can be turned into a competition, into a power play even. That's certainly what we have going on in in our last story. Mulla Nasrudine is saying, "Look who thinks he's nothing!" How can this beggar think he's nothing when nothing is the great spiritual attainment of the masters?

This shows how easy it is to think that spiritual practice is about attaining something, when actually it's about attaining nothing!

We so easily turn nothing into something. We make it a thing to search for rather than simply seeing with the mystical side of our brain. We try to define it. Try to rope it in.

What would be better, with our spiritual practices, is to take this mystical side of our brain and turn it into a luxurious garden. It doesn't need things that you can grasp. It just needs to grow. And that's the beauty of it.

There is this is part of us that sees beauty that creates beauty. This is the part of us that's simple and kind. Imagine this as a as a worldwide practice where everyone, at least once a day, stops and becomes very simple. If we could all just relax into being a human being for a moment. Slow the striving down. Slow the competition down… for just a moment, and just be.

We have such an incredible world that most of us live in. We live in incredible luxury, and we don't really enjoy it because of all this striving and striving and striving. That's the thing that's ruining the environment, you know. It's not just carbon happening all by itself. The carbon comes from all the busyness.

Why can't we just sit and enjoy? And particularly why can't we sit and enjoy each other? That would be nice.

So, take a second. Just enjoy it for a moment.

Praying on the Lake

Okay. So, there was this lake way out in the wilds. And in the middle of the lake was a small island. People started hearing rumors that there was this amazing Mystic living on this island, a holy man.

The church fathers heard about it, and they were concerned. They decided they'd better go check it out. So, they go way out in the wilds. They have a boat, and they get on the boat, and they paddle themselves out to the island.

On the island they find this scruffy old guy. He was uneducated, but he had a certain glow about him. The bishops were curious.

They asked him, "We hear rumors that you're this amazing Mystic."

The guy answers and says, "Well I don't know about that."

The Church Fathers decided to test him, so they asked, "Show us how you pray?"

The old man answered slowly, "Well. I don't know much about praying. Nobody's ever taught me how to pray."

The church fathers said, "Show us anyway. Show us the way that you are praying so that we can see."

The guy sits silently for a bit and says, "The only thing I know to do is to simply look at the beauty around me and say, "Oh existence! You are so beautiful, and so kind to contain a person such as me. Thank you. I bow before you."

The church fathers laughed, looked at him and said, "That's not a prayer! That's all wrong. We don't have a prayer anything like that."

The fellow says, "I am so sorry. Show me how to do it right."

So, they sat down and they taught him this incredibly complicated prayer. He tried it a couple of times. The church fathers thought he was doing pretty good and were satisfied with themselves. We've done our job here!

They all get back in the boat and they head off across the lake. As they're paddling across this big lake and they hear a splashing sound. They look around and here's this old guy running across the water, walking on the water. He runs up to the boat and says, "Oh stop, stop. I've already forgotten what you taught me. Could you give me that prayer again."

Simplicity in Prayer

In the end the thing that really matters is simplicity. That's what the island story is talking about. The Mystic is simply living out on the lake. The priests and the bishops come and try to teach him how to pray correctly, when he was out there just simply one with nature, one with God.

So, watch out... because we do this kind of thing all the time. This little teaching is saying to watch out for all the knowledge in your mind. All those beliefs about how you should do this correctly and you should do that correctly. Like believing you must sit in a certain way in order to meditate, or that you must think proper thoughts to get the things you want to get.

We particularly need to get rid of the beliefs of what we are trying to attain in eastern mysticism. You don't know what it is... that's why you are looking for it.

What it is you're trying to attain? It's so simple that if you knew it you would be it. If you saw even just a glimpse of it, you would be it. It's that easy to be completely one with existence. There's nothing about you that is created out of existence.

That's what E=MC2 is telling us, right? Everything comes from something. Everything is related, entwined together. Energy and matter, you and me. We are all part of one thing.

When we live there, knowing that, then simplicity is the result.

The Sound of
One Hand Clapping

What is the sound of one hand clapping? This is one of the most important Kōans given to students of Enlightenment. I have a couple of ideas about it I want to share.

I don't know for sure, you know, but it seems to me that the answer is obvious. First… what's the sound of two hands clapping?

Smack! Yes. Easy. Right?

What's the sound of one hand clapping?

It makes no sound. That the answer. It is really that simple.

So why was it given to us as a mysterious Kōan? Why have meditators contemplated this for centuries?

The Bad Side

First look at the bad side of it. I don't know if this was done on purpose, but the result of this Kōan is to turn us into forever seekers. We're told we can't figure out something

115

this easy and simple. We're told that it takes lifetimes and lifetimes and lifetimes to figure this out. The result of that belief is this never-ending quest. We become numb to the act of always seeking, never finding.

I'm challenging that idea. It's easier to find the answer than we've been told.

The Good Side.

The reason for this confusion, I think, is because these things come to us from a long, long time ago. Buddha was eight hundred BC. That was a long time ago. If you actually study history, if you study history and math, you'll find out that human beings weren't able to understand the concept of zero for centuries. We didn't have the concept of zero, of nothing, for many centuries of our recorded history.

It wasn't until the 1300s, 1400s, that the concept of zero started to be understood in the western word. Before that it was only mystics mentioning nothing, or zero. The mathematical idea of zero is only a few centuries old. It only recently started being used in math and commerce.

Way back in Buddha's time they hadn't figured it out yet. Zero was the thing of mysticism. Grasping the idea of nothing without the numerical concept of zero was incredibly difficult.

Today it seems obvious to us. We were taught about zero in kindergarten, right? We've known about it our whole lives. It seems like such an obvious thing. An everyday thing…

you know: ten, nine, eight, seven, six, five, four, three, two, one… zero. To us it's just a number

We even know how to go negative of zero. What grade did we learn that? Was it in third grade? So, zero, to us, the idea of zero, is a normal thing. Way back in the time of Buddha it was mysterious and unknown: the idea that there could be nothing?

It's not a natural human thing to come up with the idea of zero. It's something that we have to figure out and be taught. Just think about it. Imagine that you lived a long time ago. You're a farmer, or maybe you're a hunter gatherer, and you look out and you see three deer. Count them: one, two, three. Easy. People learned to count a long, long, long time ago.

But what if you look out and you don't see any deer at all? You might think, "I'm hungry. There aren't any deer here. Let's go find some deer." But you don't think there are zero deer.

Zero as an actual concept took centuries to come into our societies. The Mayan culture, apparently, had the idea of zero. That was one of the reasons their mathematics, and their calendar was so amazing.

But go back to the to the place where this Kōan came from. What's the sound of one hand clapping?

It's nothing.

You can get it. I can get it easily today. We can grasp the idea of zero, the idea of nothing. We can conceive that there's nothing there. If there is only one hand to clap it makes no sound.

Imagine Buddha, and his monks, trying to sort it out. They didn't have the idea of zero and were some of the first people to start contemplating the idea of nothing. Of nothingness itself.

Even with our minds today we can experience it as mysterious. Stop for a sec. Pause and visualize nothing. It is mind boggling.

What is nothing? What is zero? Look deeply at it. You'll feel your mind stretched to new places. Or maybe a better way to describe it is that you must use a different part of your mind to see it. You can't really see it. Of course, because it's nothing. The exercise is more like letting the thinking part of you rest and letting the visualizing part of your mind expand.

And be careful... I'm not saying to think about nothing, as in don't think about anything. I'm saying, think about "nothing."

Your mind doesn't have anything to grasp onto when you really think about nothing. It's a mystical experience.

Today in our society we have this idea of zero. We know it as a thing. It's everywhere. In eight hundred BC there was no such thing. One of the stories about Buddha is that he was so brilliant he could count to a thousand. Big whoop we'd say today. First graders can count to a thousand today if they had the patience. But just think how hard counting was before the number zero existed. You couldn't just count up like we do. You couldn't go: one, two, three, four, five, six, seven, eight, nine, and then make a leap into double digits.

The number ten for us is a one and a zero. Right? When you are counting you hit that and keep going up. Easy Peasy. It even gets easier when you get to 20. Just add the numbers in one by one: 21, 22, 23… Same thing with 30: 31, 32, 33.

It's just as easy in the hundreds: 121, 122, 123… Just as easy in the thousands: 1021, 1022, 1023… It's an easy logical progression. If you have enough time you could count to the billions. Quadrillions.

But back in Buddha's time if you wanted to count from one to a thousand every single one of those numbers had a different name. We have a little bit of that now because when we get up to ten then we've got eleven and twelve, instead of saying oneteen, twoteen, thirteen. When we get to 20 it starts hitting the logical progression of 21, 22, 23. But imagine how crazy it would be if every number from one to a thousand was a different word. It would take a genius to count to a thousand.

Anyway. The point is that way back when this Kōan was first brought forward it was the very beginning of trying to figure out this mystical idea of nothing, of zero.

What's the sound of one hand clapping? You know the answer. It's nothing. There's no sound.

What's the sound of two hands clapping? Clap! We all know it.

What's the sound of a thousand hands clapping? You know that one! It's like a ball game or a concert. It's just that easy.

This is one of the reasons why I think people today are so much closer to grasping the secret of who you are. Because we have the whole history of human knowledge behind us. This thing inside you, this thing that you think is you, that you think is this separate thing from everything else doesn't exist. It's nothing. If you can actually look inside, with complete honesty, and see this nothing. Then you hear this sound of one hand clapping.

There's your mystery right there. Looking at zero, contemplating it, immediately calms down the thinking mind. It puts you in a place of the now. It puts you into just being alive. You can understand zero. See the hum of it. You're still alive. You can see Zero. You are seeing from who you really are. That zero. It's huge. It's nothing.

Can't Talk About Nothing

You can't really talk about nothing because the very act of talking is something. The very act of giving nothing a word, naming it nothing, or zero, turns it into something. Both in in the words that I'm saying and in what you're hearing me say.

But what if the collective wisdom of humanity that has brought us to this point has given us the key to unlocking Eastern Mysteries very simply. What if we realize that it was a long time ago when these stories were first created, when Buddha had his first experience of nothing. What if we have learned so much since then that we now actually have ways to understand it?

We know what zero is. We can grasp this idea of 'nothing' that used to be completely mysterious to Mystics.

Looking at Nothing

It still is very mystical and wonderful to sit and simply experience nothing, because the biggest part of your brain, of your physical brain, is activated when words go silent. Words are important, yes. Thoughts, logic, concepts, are important. But these are only a small part of our ability to see and experience life.

So, what if this really is the key to understanding our completely integrated self? These simple things we know today. Things that Mystics thousands of years ago struggled with.

What if we start using this knowledge. You know what zero is. You know that matter comes from energy and energy comes from matter. You know that everything is related to everything else. Experiment with it. Experience it for a little while. Unlock it.

What if you are that nothingness. What does that feel like? What do you see?

Yes

When I saw the
connection to all. I laughed.

Wondrous to think
I could eat without teeth
or breathe without air.

The blanket of trees,
roots deep in the ground,
shoots the ocean water
under bird's wings.

The husband's love fills the breast with infant's milk.
Laughter and tears burst
from the same belly.

Burn through the
dust, my friend, the reflection looking
for itself.
See with your own
eyes and eat with your tongue.

Dash the stingy heart.
Love is *your* gift.
Say yes.

122

Teacups

And finally. We have to conclude with a Zen story that everyone has heard of. It's the one with the teacup.

A man goes and finds a master. Usually, the story is embellished with a tale of adventure where the guy climbs a huge mountain and gets up to the top. He finally gets there and asks for enlightenment. The master sits him down and says, "Let's have a cup of tea."

He starts pouring and pouring and pouring the tea until the teacup fills up, and then starts overflowing. And he keeps pouring and he keeps pouring with tea spilling all around. Finally, the seeker cries out, "Stop it's full! You can't put any more in there because it's full!"

The master stops and says, "Exactly. You are like this teacup. You are so full of ideas. So full of beliefs of what you think spirituality should be, that there is no way that I can put even a drop more in there.

We have to empty you out first.

Don't Fill Up

I close this series of Zen stories with a final warning that comes from the last story we told about the teacup. The master is filling and filling the filling the cup until there's no room for anything else. The teacup represents all the books you've read, including this one.

Don't let these stories fill you up with knowledge. The mind always craves knowledge and power.

Instead let these Zen stories empty you, each with their "stopping point." The effectiveness of these stories is their ability to create pictures in your mind that don't attach words. Stories, that defy concepts.

Let the stories sit in your mind's eye and forget the details as much as possible. Don't fill your cup. Let it be empty, so that as you walk forward life enters you, wisdom grows in you. So that you know who you are in this world.

Always know that the world needs you fully awake.

Printed in Great Britain
by Amazon